5-STEP EASY EAR TRAINING

for

PIANO

5-STEP EASY EAR TRAINING for PIANO

Elsa Harris

5-Step Easy Ear Training
Copyright © 2024 by Elsa Harris

Printed in the United States of America

ISBN: 979-8-218-32073-7

CONTENT

Acknowledgement

I would like to take this time to thank every proof-reader for their input to this book. It was very, very helpful. Much thanks to the following:

Rev. Karl B Wilson - Former pastor of Bryn Mawr Community Church in Chicago. Also, is a licensed funeral director and board certified counselor for A.A. Rayner Funeral Home in Chicago

Dr. Wilma Turner - Tuskegee University Grad., Former Elementary School teacher for CPS, author of two books: More Than Conquerors and Racism in America.

Steven Dolins - Former professor at Bradley University, remains as Computer Science and Chair Emeritus of Computer Science, Producer and owner of Sirens Records in Chicago.

Joan Hutchinson - Min. of Music at Congregational Church of Oak Park. long-standing member of CAMTA (Chicago Area Music Teachers Association), former piano teacher. Graduate of Boston University and also American Conservatory of Music.

Who is Elsa Harris?

Minister Elsa Harris is a gospel musician, arranger, music teacher, and a native Chicagoan. she has studied music at the Chicago conservatory of music, Vander-Cook College of Music, with a four year scholarship. Her studies were interrupted by the opportunity to travel with international singer-songwriter Jessy Dixon as his pianist and background singer.

the Jessy Dixon singers toured with Paul Simon, and that relationship lasted for eight years. Elsa traveled with the Jessy Dixon singers all over the world. Elsa Harris and Jessy Dixon's relationship lasted 50 years until Dixon's death.

Elsa continued her musical studies at Loop jr. College, and Sherwood Conservatory. She has had extensive training in classical music. Her love for God and for church music led her in the direction of different genres of church music, from traditional hymns to contemporary rock gospel.

Elsa is an ordained elder under the spiritual covering of the Liberty Temple Full Gospel Church of Chicago, Illinois, giving her the title of Minister Elsa Harris. Minister Harris' accomplishments are too numerous to name. During the 50 years with Jessy Dixon, some of the tours included Chuck Colson's Prison Ministry, Billy Graham Ministry, Pat Boon shows, PTL, 700 Club, and many others.

She has trained numerous choirs in Norway, Sweden, Denmark,

Romania, England, Canada, Finland, Ireland, Switzerland, East and West Germany, Africa, and many of the islands from Bermuda to Jamaica, Trinidad and Tobago.

She is a member of the Chicago Music Teachers Association and The Music Teachers National Association. She was recently interviewed on PBS channel 11, Chicago tonight show for a seven minute documentary about her life. Her many awards include selected as a Gospel Legend at the Gospel Fest of Chicago in 2012. She was honored by the Edwin and Walter Hawkins Music and Arts Organization, and so much more.

INTRODUCTION: What Does it Mean to Play by Ear?

To play by ear means to play, on a musical instrument, what you hear in your head. It can be either your own composition or someone else's composition on a recording or live. It's about re-creating what you imagined that you just heard. First, you create a mental memory of what you hear. It could be what you heard on one or several musical instruments. Sometimes, it's best to start with just focusing on the vocal or instrumental solo of a song. This would be where the melody line is. A melody line is the part of a song that's easiest for anyone to sing along. The melody of a song can stand alone, without any harmony help. It's where the lyrics of the song can be sung as a solo. In this chapter, I will explain how to use your memory to create and/or re-create the music that you heard in your head.

I suggest you start your ear-training on the piano first. It helps to develop your musical ear on a keyboard instrument of at least 60 keys or more in width. It is easiest to start with picking out easy songs that stay within a musical scale, using just one finger.

What is This Book About?

This book is about learning how to play strictly by using your musical ear. I have decided to use only the musical alphabet to illustrate how this is possible. The piano keyboard is the main musical instrument of all musical instruments. I strongly recommend learning fundamentals about it first. The use of note reading will not be necessary at this stage.

This approach will show you how to develop your musical ear to hear scales and chords, which, in my opinion, are the two main ingredients in all of music. I will also demonstrate how to improvise with fill-ins, bass walks, chord patterns, duplications with both hands, and more. Every chapter in this book will be immediately followed by exercises that will better help you to understand how scales and chords work in an actual song. It's all about how to find the key, find the chords, and then proceed to play the song, almost immediately. Most church musicians are finding themselves in that predicament only too often. At least, that is what I have personally observed in most African American churches.

Please understand, I was not born with a fully developed musical ear. I had to work at it. And so will some of you. To some, it will become easier and quicker than others. But keep practicing, and you will begin to see and hear the results sooner than you think. Your comprehensive level will begin to excel, by leaps and bounds as you proceed to embrace this method. It's up to you to stay focused and follow through with the exercises. So let's get started!

I would like to take this time to salute all church musicians who have gone through the trauma of having to find the key, find the chords, and play the song immediately, on the spot for, say, a guest soloist, or the pastor's favorites song, in any given religious service. It could be nerve wrecking, especially when it's required of the musician to play in public with only a quick second notice. The musician must have some knowledge of scales and chords to successfully pull that off at a moment's notice.

If you are one of those musicians who have experienced these kinds of traumatic moments, then, this book is especially for you. You might be gifted to play piano/keyboards, but do you know and understand what key or key family you are playing in??? This book is designed with you in mind.

CHAPTER ONE: Getting Familiar With the Keyboard

First of all, it is important to familiarize yourself with the keyboard. The size or width at this point is not so important. Since you will only concentrate on the middle part of the keyboard, the width could be between 40 and 60 keys wide for beginners. To start, you need to recognize the order of the keys on the keyboard.

a) **(Finding the white keys)** There are only 7 letters in the alphabet that are used in music. They are: A, B, C, D, E, F, & G. There is a Biblical reference here. The Bible clearly shows that the number 7 is the number of completion. So, the first 7 letters of the alphabet are all we really need. All the music in the world uses, basically, just these 7 letters, or keys! It might seem strangely impossible, but it's true! Since the Almighty Creator is a God of order, you will notice a definite numerical order of keys and letters as we progress throughout this book. Look closely at the keyboard diagram below.

You will see a definite order of black and white keys that repeats in every grouping of 12 keys. They are the distance of ½ step apart in pitch from each other.

Exercise #1

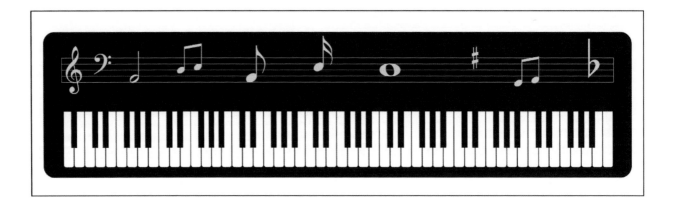

Pick any key and, with an upward motion, play black and white keys in succession, and you will notice that after the 12th key, the pattern will repeat itself, only higher. The number 12 is the Biblical number of government or organization. You will certainly appreciate that later in this book.

You will notice that the keys on your left side represent the lower end of the piano, and the keys on your right side represent the higher end. If you play the lowest white key on an 88-keyboard piano, the lowest white key will always be the first letter of the alphabet, A. The next white key is B, then C, D, E, F, & G. That's seven different keys. The next key will be another A, then B, C, D, E, F, & G again. This pattern will continue in this alphabetical order all the way to the highest end of the keyboard and end on a very, very high C.

Exercise #2

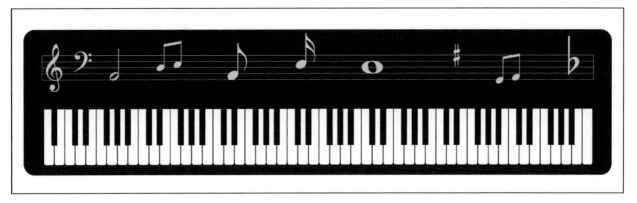

See if you can name all the white keys on the keyboard by starting with the lowest key. If your keyboard isn't 88 keys wide, then use the black keys to help you name the white keys. Black keys also have names, that will be explained in more detail in a later chapter. But for now, they can be beneficial with finding and memorizing the white keys. The musical keyboard is a universal set up. So, it is crucial to understand it and memorize the order.

b) **(Finding the black keys)** The black keys are in groups of alternating 2's and 3's. They will help you with finding and recognizing the groups of white keys. As the diagram indicates, the white keys have letter-names in alphabetical order. I will explain how that relates to the names of the black keys later. But for now, locate all the groups of 2 black keys, then all the groups of 3 black keys. All keyboards are set up in that way. As you listen to each group, your ear is being trained to recognize high, low, and middle pitches on the keyboard.

Exercise #3

Use the groups of black keys to help you find the white keys by the correct letter-names. Observe the diagram below.

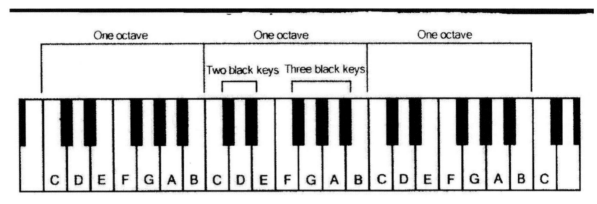

[Diagram used with Yamaha's permission]

You will notice that on the immediate left side of all the two group black keys, is a white key named C.

Exercise #4

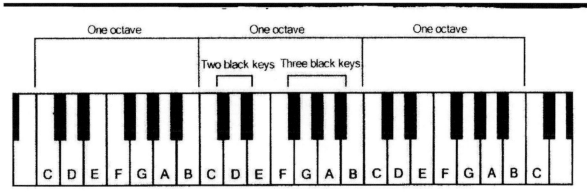

Once you are sure you have found a C, then try to find all the Cs on the keyboard. Your ear will hear a higher C sound every 8 keys up. Then do the same with Ds, Es, Fs, and so forth. The Gs, As, and Bs are in between and around the group of three black keys. It's easy to find and play the keys if you think in alphabetical order. How many A's, B's, C's, etc., were you able to locate? Now that you have found all your white keys by name, locate the C that is most in the middle of the keyboard.

Remember, it will be on the left side of the group of 2 black keys, always, always. Now let's examine how that works, starting with the construction of a musical scale.

CHAPTER TWO: The Musical Scale

In this chapter, you will learn how to construct a Major scale and how to pick out the melody of a song using your ear and the scale only. It is important to recognize and appreciate the distance between two tones. Some are high, some are low, and some are somewhat in the middle of a melody.

There are 12 Major scales that have at least 3 fundamental functions: Major, Minor, and Chromatic. In this book, I chose to only cover the Major scale, just to keep it simple for now. The other scales will be covered in the next book (Intermediate Level).

a) What is a Major scale?

A Major scale is a succession of 8 tones in a musical alphabetical order. The number 8 in the Bible represents the number of new beginnings. First, let's consider the order.

Let's start with the C Major scale. It is the only scale, out of all 12, that is played on **all white keys.** The first key of the scale is the actual name of the scale: C, D, E, F, G. A. B. C. The 8th key is always the same name as the first key. They should sound the same when played together, only one is a high C, and the other is a lower C. Every eighth key should help you remember that the scale is about to repeat itself higher.

Exercise #1

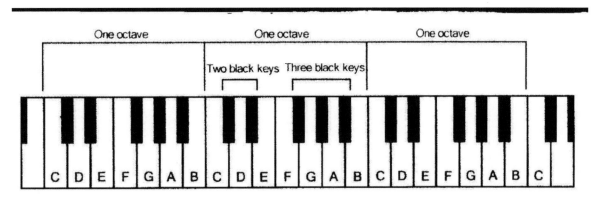

[Diagram used with Yamaha's permission]

b)　How to Construct a Major Scale

Play the C Major Scale and listen carefully to the pitch of each key as it gets higher and higher. You might have heard of the solfeggio (do, re, mi, fa, sol, la, ti, do), the Italian music method used to teach pitch relativity. C is do, D is re, E is mi, F is fa, and so forth. Or, you might consider counting upward in the scale with the Arabic numbers like this: C is 1, D is 2, E is 3, F is 4, and so forth. Use whichever method is most comfortable for you.

Exercise #2

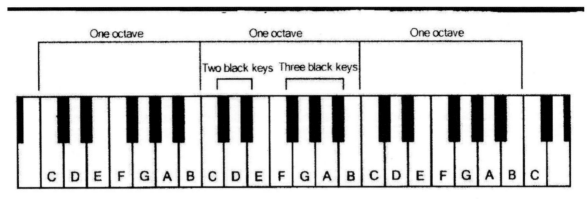

Practice the C Major Scale while saying or singing along with the solfeggio or the regular numbers.

c)   Pick out a Melody

Another good exercise would be to mix up the letters to recognize how far one pitch is from another.

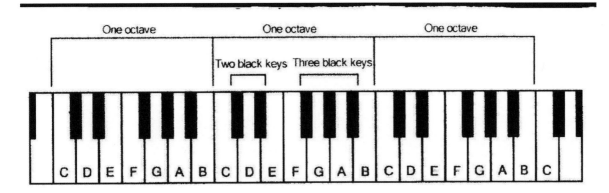

(Ex. – C, E, G, A, G, E, C) also, recognize when the pitch stays the same. (Ex. – EEE, EEE, EGC, D E). This simple exercise will help in developing the ear to pick out simple melodies of a song you may already know, such as:

1. Mary Had A Little Lamb
2. London Bridge Is Falling Down
3. Twinkle, Twinkle, Little Star
4. Oh, How I Love Jesus
5. What A Mighty God We Serve
6. My Country Tis of Thee
7.   Jingle Bells

Just to name a few . . .

These songs use only the keys in the C Major scale. With a little practice, they should be easy for you to pick out with your right hand only.

Exercise #4

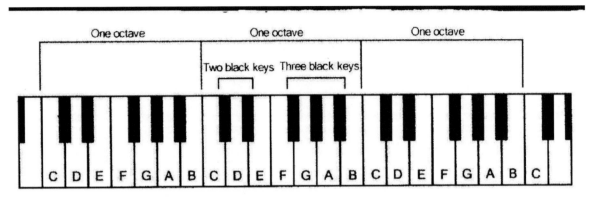

Try it. Notice that some songs start on, either the first tone of the scale, the 3rd tone of the scale or, the 5th tone of the scale. These are the 3 main key pitches that most songs start on. Keeping this in mind should help you find the starting note for each song. In the following exercises, I have already provided that for you. Just find the missing notes in the first 10 songs and NAME THAT TUNE! With the next 10 songs you will need to fill in more missing letters to finish the songs. Have fun!!!

FILL IN BLANKS
AND LYRICS

SONG #1:

E D D D E E _ D D _ E G _

_____

E D C _ E E E E D D _ _ _

_____

SONG #2

CCGGAA_ FFEEDD_

_____

GGFFEED G_F_E_D

_____

CCGGA_G F_EEDD_

_____

Song # 3

G A G F _ F G _ E F _ F G

_____

G A G _ _ F _ D G E _ _

_____

SONG #4

E E D E C _ D D C D _ G

_____

E E D E_ _ E D F E D__

_____

SONG # 5

E E E E E _ E G C D __

_____

F F F F F E _ e e E D D E _ G

_____

E E E E E E E G _ _ E

_____

F F F F F E E e e G G F __ __

_____

SONG # 6

C C D __ cd E E F __ dc

D C B C

G G G __ fe F F F __ ed

E fedc __ fg af E __ __

SONG # 7

CEFG CEF__ CEF__

ECE__ EEDC CE G

GGF EF__ ECD__

SONG # 8

c C G gg a A G

c C G __ __ f E D

c C G __ __ a A G

F E C d D __

SONG # 9

E E F G G F E D __ __ D E

__ d d   E E F G G F E D __

__ D E __ c c

SONG # 10

GEG GEG AGFE__EF

ef G C ccc c _ _ _ G

G D D F__ __ C

SONG # 11

*Write the correct melody line notes over the lyrics.

G   G   E   G   E C

He's got the whole world, in His

Hand He's got the whole world,

In His hand, He's got the whole

 world, in His hand He's got the

whole world in His hand.

Song # 12

C   C   D   E   F

Some - times in our lives,

We all have pain – we all

have sorrow, but, if we are

wise, we know that there's

always to- mor – row.

SONG # 13

C   D   E F   F   F   C   D E   E

This land is your land, this land is my land,

From California, to the New York island.

From the Redwood Forest, to the Gulf Stream

 waters

This land was made for you and me.

SONG # 14

```
E    D    C    E    D    C
```

Three blind mice, three blind mice

See how they run, see how they run

They all ran after the farmer's wife,

She cut off their tails with a carving knive

Did you e-ver see such a sight in your life as

Three blind mice.

SONG # 15

C   C D   E   C   C D   E

This is the day, this is the day

That the Lord has made that the Lord has made

I will rejoice, I will rejoice

And be glad in it, and be glad in it.

This is the day that the Lord has made.

I will rejoice and be glad in it.

This is the day, this is the day, that the Lord, has made.

SONG # 16

E E E D C   E E E D C

Victory is mine, victory is mine

Victory today is mine.

I told Satan, get thee behind,

Victory today is mine

SONG # 17

G   G G   E C   A G

What a mighty God we serve,

What a mighty God we serve,

Angels bow before Him,

Heaven and earth a -dore Him

What a mighty God we serve.

SONG # 18

C C D E C E D

Yankee Doodle went to town,

Riding on a po-ny

Stuck a feather in his hat

And called it macaro-ni

SONG #19

G G   A A G fe

We shall o-ver come, We shall o-ver come

We shall o-ver come some day

Deep in my heart, I do believe

We shall over come some day

SONG # 20

E D C   F E D C

Oh the blood of Je—sus,

Oh the blood of Je—sus,

Oh, the blood of Je—sus,

It washes white as snow.

CHAPTER THREE: Chords

One of the most basic building blocks of music are chords. Chords have letter- names that are built in a specific order, with one of the letters actually naming the chord. Now that you have formed the C Major scale with letters, let's begin to form chords using only the letters in that scale. Here's how:

a) Building Chords

Notice the chord chart below. This is Chord Family Diagram #1

THE "C" CHORD FAMILY

	Major (X)							Minor ( )
2nd Inversion 6/4	g C e							
1st Inversion 6/3	e g C							
Root	C e g							
Scale	C	D	E	F	G	A	B
RN Scale	I	ii	iii	IV	V	vi	vii

The first seven letters of the scale **should** be written in the bottom boxes, one capital letter per box, in alphabetical order, starting with C. The boxes above each letter will be used to spell what is called a triad, a 3-tone chord. To build a chord, on each tone of a given scale, simply skip- a-letter, starting with the letter that names the chord. For example, the C Major chord is built by using the letters C E and G. If you stick to the letters only in that scale, you will always build accurately, in alphabetical order, no matter what scale you build on. More about that later.

I stumbled upon this formula while on break at work one day. I continued to try it on other scales, and to my amazement, it was always accurate!

The second letter in the scale is D. To build a chord on the D tone, starting with D, just skip to F and then to A. Got it?

Exercise #1

For example, see if you can finish building all the chords on the C Major scale using the chart above.

Chords are born into the chord family in a specific order: The first chord, C Major, is a happy sounding chord. It is called a *Major* chord for a specific reason. I will explain how they are mathematically built later. The second chord, D *minor*, is a sad sounding chord. It is called minor for a specific reason as well. The third chord, E, is also born into the family as a minor chord. The fourth and fifth chords are happy chords, born Major, but the sixth chord is born minor. The last different chord out of the 7 is born diminished. I call it the "unfinished diminished" because it needs to be settled, mostly by the Home chord, which is the I chord.

There is a reasonable explanation for that as well. Just hold on! All will be explained in time. Right now, just observe the order and the set- up. Listen to the different sounds of each chord.

Exercise #2

In the bottom row of chords, write the 3 letters that spell the chord name of the letter below it. Write all three letters in the box directly above the capital letter that names the chord. You may write the 3 letters, horizontally, vertically, or diagonally, but always stick to the same order for uniformity.

You will notice that a chord can be played three different ways: **Root position**, where the note that names the chord is in the lowest note position (C-e-g), **First inversion**, where the note that names the chord has been flipped to the top of it (e-g-C), while the other 2 notes slide down in position, and lastly, the **Second inversion**, where the named chord note is now the middle letter in position (g-C-e).

Now play all 3 positions of the C chord up and down a few times. Then, continue to build and play the rest of the chords you have built in the C chord family. Notice the mathematical accuracy. Also, notice that the spelling of each chord may change in position, but not in spelling. One chord can be played in three different ways by using the same letter- names, but by using other keys on the keyboard that have those same letter-names.

In other words, a C Major chord is a C Major chord, all over the world, and the spelling does not change, EVER! You could even stretch the spelling by playing a low C, a middle E, and a very high G, or mix them up any way you choose. It is still a C Major chord, forever. That's just the way Almighty God created it! How fantastic is that!!!?

As you will notice, chords are born into the Major Chord Family in a specific order. The first chord, which always names the key a song is in, is always Major, the second and third chords are always born minor, the fourth and fifth chords are always born Major, the sixth chord minor, and the seventh chord, always the unfinished diminished. For now, we will only use the Major (happy) chords, I = 1, IV = 4, and V = 5 chords. There are two schools of teaching on how to identify these chord names: **The Nashville notation**, commonly used by professional studio musicians, and t**he Roman Numeral notation**, more commonly used across musical genres today. I prefer to use the Roman Numeral approach to identify the chords in any chord family. So, in the C chord Family, I is

the C chord, IV is the F chord, and V is the G chord.

Practice these 3 chords, in the 3 positions until well memorized.

b)   Learning (Primary) Close Chord Patterns

In the illustration below, I indicate a color-coded system (Green, Yellow & Red). These are the colors of the stop and go lights that must be observed while driving. The green color used in the first Root position chord box at the very left-hand corner (C chord) is mostly used when starting to chord a song. It serves as a starting point.

Before chording a song, let's familiarize the close chord progressions generally used to accompany a simple song like Mary Had A Little Lamb. Go to the IV column and find the closest chord to the root position C chord (Green box). Use this simple formula: Same Letter,

Same Position (match the same letter(s) which stay in the same position while changing from one chord to the next). Ex: the I (root C chord) is spelled

Ceg. The spelling of the closest IV chord must have at least one letter in common with the I chord that is in the same position. It could be either the root position, the 1st inversion, or the 2nd inversion of the IV chord, but there is only one correct answer.

Did you find it? The correct answer is the 2nd inversion box. It is spelled cFa. This box should also be color-coded green. The letter the two chords share in common is C. Try playing the root C chord, then playing the 2nd inversion F chord. You will find that the letter C stays in the same position with this simple chord progression, while the e-g moves up to f-a. The whole point is to keep chord progressions as close as possible.

Now, let's try matching the same I Root chord with the closest V chord. See if you can find the same letter in the same position on the keyboard. When you find it, color-code the correct V chord box.

Check it by playing the two chords back and forth [don't turn to the page after the blank sheet until after completing the assignment, as it has the answer sheet].

	Major (X)						Minor ( )
2nd Inversion 6/4	g C e			c F a	d G b		
1st Inversion 6/3	e g C			a c F	b d G		
Root	C e g			F a c	G b d		
Scale	C	D	E	F	G	A	B
RN Scale	I	ii	iii	IV	V	vi	vii

THE "C" CHORD FAMILY

	Major (X)	ii	iii	IV	V	vi	Minor ( )
2nd Inversion 6/4	g C e			c F a	d G b		
1st Inversion 6/3	e g C			a c F	b d G		
Root	C e g	D	E	F a c	G b d	A	B
Scale	C	D	E	F	G	A	B
RN Scale	Ⓘ	ii	iii	ⒾⓋ	Ⓥ	vi	vii

c)   Close Chord Patterns & Exercises

#1 – I, IV, I, IV, I, IV, I
#2 – I, V, I, V, I, V, I
#3 – I, IV, I, V, I, IV, I, V, I, V, I, V, I

After you have mastered the green boxes, then try and fill in the Yellow boxes, and then lastly the red boxes the same way. If you get the green and yellow boxes correct, the red boxes will automatically be correct.

(repeat each exercise as needed.)

THE <u>"C"</u> CHORD FAMILY

	Major (X)						Minor ( )
2nd Inversion 6/4	g C e			c F a	d G b		
1st Inversion 6/3	e g C			a c F	b d G		
Root	C e g			F a c	G b d		
Scale	C	D	E	F	G	A	B
RN Scale	I	ii	iii	IV	V	vi	vii

THE "C" CHORD FAMILY

	Major (X)			Scale	RN Scale
2nd Inversion 6/4	g C e				
1st Inversion 6/3	e g C				
Root	C e g			C	(I)
				D	ii
				E	iii
	e F a	a c F	F a c	F	(IV)
	d G b	b d G	G b d	G	(V)
				A	vi
Minor ( )				B	vii

CHAPTER FOUR: Playing With Two Hands

To play with two hands, you must start by playing the one-finger melody with the right hand only. (Remember, this is Book One, so we will keep it very simple and very basic for now.)

a) Coordination

Once you feel comfortable enough with playing the melody of a short song, almost by memory, then, and only then, are you ready to add chords to the melody with your left hand.

The illustration below will show you when and where to place the left-hand chords in the song. The boxed letters, placed over certain words, indicate where the left hand should play along with the melody of the song in the right hand. It's very important to place the chords with certain words in the song. Try playing the songs below with two hands.

Exercise #1

First, begin to practice the I, IV, & V chords with your left hand on the keyboard directly under the middle C area. Remember to keep the chords in a close progression. Once you have memorized these 3 close chord progressions, you may begin to add the right-hand melody of a simple easy song like Mary Had A Little Lamb. Some of you will figure this out right away. Others may need to play the C Major scale a few times to keep the key in mind. By now, you should have figured out that the song starts on the 3rd tone of the C Major scale (E). With your left hand, play the I chord (C) with that tone. Below are two short song illustrations to get you started. Try playing them (refer to the songlist at the end of this book for more challenging melodies and chords to pick out).

On the left side of each line in the song, are letters explaining what the particular line stands for. M - melody line, L - lyrics to the song, and C - chords placed directly under the lyric and melody line. If you keep this in mind, while following the directions, it should all come together very quickly and easy.

Mary Had A Little Lamb

M) E D C D E E E

L) Mary had a little lamb,

C) [C]   [C]

M) D D D   E G G

L) little lamb, little lamb,

C) [G]   [C]

M) E D   C D E E   E

L) Mary had a little lamb,

C) [C]   [C]

M) E D   D E   D C

L) his fleece was white as snow

C) [G]   [C]

NOTE: The melody line is the same for the following verses. See if you can match the melody for each verse, with the lyrics below.

Vs.2) Everywhere that Mary went, Mary went, Mary went, everywhere that Mary went, the lamb was sure to go.

Vs.3) Followed her to school one day, school one day, school one day, followed her to school one day which was against the rule.

Vs.4) Made the children laugh and play, laugh and play, laugh and play. Made the children laugh and play to see a lamb at school.

Oh When The Saints

M) C E F G C E F G

L) *Oh when the saints, go marching in,*

C)   C   C

M) C E F G E C E D

L) *Oh when the saints go marching in,*

C)   C   G

M) E E D C C E G G G F

L) *Oh Lord I want, to be, in that number,*

C)   C   F

M) E F G E C D C

L) *When the saints go marching in.*

C)   C   C G C

b) Recognizing Chord Patterns

You will notice that certain chords sound better in certain places than others. It's okay to experiment with different chords until you hear what sounds best to your ear. After all, this is EAR training. Since the I, IV, and V chords seem to show up in so many songs, after a little practice, you will begin to recognize where the best chords should go.

Chord patterns usually show up when a melodic phrase repeats itself. Look for them in "Mary Had A Little Lamb." The chord patterns on lines 1 & 3 are the same. Also, on lines 2 & 4. Observing chord patterns will help you practice and memorize any song.

London Bridge

M) G   A   G   F   E F   G

L) *London Bridge is falling down,*

C) [C]   [C]

M) D   E   F   E   F   G

L) *falling down, falling   down.*

C) [G]   [C]

M) G   A   G   F E F   G

L) *London Bridge is falling down,*

C) [C]   [C]

M)   D   G   E C

L) *my fair lady*

C) [G]   [C]

Twinkle, Twinkle, Little Star

M) C   C   G   G   A A   G

L) Twinkle,   Twinkle   little   star

C) [C]   [C]   [F]   [C]

M)   F   F   E   E   D   D   C

L)   How   I   wonder   what   you   are

C) [F]   [C]   [G]   [C]

M)   G   G F   F   E   E   D

L)   Up   above   the   world   so   high

C) [C]   [G]   [C]   [G]

M)   G   G   F   F   E   D

L)   Like   a   diamond   in   the   sky,

C) [C]   [F]   [C]   [G]

M)   C   C   G   G   A A   G

L)   Twinkle,   twinkle   little   star

C) [C]   [C]   [F]   [C]

M)   F   F   E   E   D   D   C

L)   How   I   wonder   what   you   are.

C) [F]   [C]   [G]   [C]

Oh How I Love Jesus

M)   E   E   D E   C   C

L) *Oh, How I Love Je - sus*

C) C   C C

M)   D   D   C D   E   G

L) Oh, How I Love Je - sus

C) G   C C

M)

L) Oh, How I Love Je - sus

C) C   C C

M)

L) Because, He first, loved me.

C) G   C G C

---

c)   Playing with Rhythm

Songs usually fall in 2 rhythmic categories: 3/4 and 4/4 time 3/4 time = 1,2,3 1,2,3   1,2,3 1,2,3 and 4/4 time = 1,2,3,4 1,2,3,4 1,2,3,4 1,2,3,4. The emphasis is strongly on #1. For 3/4 time, you can practice this by patting with your foot or hand to the thigh, for the #1 beat. And then clapping on #s 2 & 3, counting aloud. For 4/4 time, simply pat the foot or thigh on #1 and #3, and clap your hands on #s 2 & 4. Since songs can be either in a slow, medium, or fast beat, just practice each tempo either faster or slower (more about time signatures, tempos, and beats, in Book 2).

Exercise #2

I challenge you to feel the rhythm of each song by either, patting your foot, clapping your hands, nodding your head to the beat, etc. You will be pleasantly surprised at how much rhythm you instinctively possess, on a subconscious level. Just think for a moment, about songs you have heard on TV, radio, recordings, etc., or while at a live concert or church service. Just "go with the flow" and enjoy!

CHAPTER FIVE: Recognizing Song Structure

Song structure is mostly referred to by some as form and analyses. It involves how well you can observe and differentiate between the verses, choruses, bridge, if any, and endings.

a) How many times does each section repeat, if at all? Does the song change keys (modulate)?

Can you separate the vocals from the instrumentation? Does the speed or rhythm of the song change at any time? These are questions that could and should be answered before you compose or learn someone else's song. It would make it so much easier to comprehend, then practice, and finally memorize, if necessary.

b) Improvisation

Most piano students are so eager to play all the riffs, runs, and fill- ins before they even have a song structure or even a decent melody line. Yes, those things do dress up a song, but like anything else, you need structure before you can put a roof or siding on a building. You need all the ingredients that go into baking a cake or pie before you put the finishing touches on top. And so it is with dressing up a song. Always get the basic chord structure and form of the song down first before trying to add the coloring that you might hear in your head. I will attempt to introduce some easy fill-ins, riffs, and runs that I think you might be hearing in your head, that will suit the song.

Exercises #1

For instance, there is the option of making rhythm with your left-hand chords as beat fill-ins. You must feel comfortable enough and coordinated enough to do so. Then, there is chord duplication in the right hand that is usually played one, two, and maybe three octaves higher than the first time, just to fill in extra time between phrases.

Exercise #2

Also, to break up, or rock your chords by playing each note separately and then together, is another way of giving the song a different color, or flavor. If you have a keyboard with the drums attachment, it would be a good thing to practice playing with the drums to help you play with a better rhythm and to encourage your creativity in this area.

c)   Intros and Endings

The introduction to a song could be, maybe, the last phrase of the song, or the first phrase, or part of it. Or, it could be totally different. Usually, the intro can be found somewhere in the song. Its purpose is to capture the listening ear by identifying. For example: G G C F E - D - C, is the ending melody line to the song "We Shall Overcome". It can be used as a short introduction to identify the song. Another example is: G G A G E D C - A (lower), G(lower), C E D B C. Can you guess the name of this song? Try before looking at the answer.

Answer: "What A Friend We Have In Jesus". It also serves as a good identifying introduction when played along with the chords, of course. If you find this to be true in a song you are learning, or composing, it should make the melody and chords easier to learn.

Endings can be as follows: repeating the last phrase, or part of the phrase that belongs at the end of the song. Sometimes, it could also be the beginning intro repeated or some part of the chorus or verse. **For example**: G G C F E -

D - C, the same line used as an Intro, can now be used as a repeated ending, sometimes referred to as the Vamp. The Vamp usually repeats until further directed, but at the end of the repeating phrase, a VI chord is added to confirm the turn around. In the key of C, that would be an A minor, or A major chord. I call it the "turn- around" chord. The same applies to the Vamp for "What A Friend We Have In Jesus". G (lower) - C E D C B C, then VI chord, and repeat. One other way to Vamp an ending which is very popular in Gospel music: play I chord to IV chord over and over, as directed, and then end on the I chord. Example: C chord to F chord over and over, then end on C chord.

Whatever it takes to drive the point home is permissible. This is a good place to add improvisation such as, duplicating the last chord upward by inversions or by octaves, either as a solid chord or a broken one, with sustain pedal for slower endings.

Exercise #3

Below is a list of categorized songs that you are encouraged to try picking out the melody first, using the C major scale mainly, then try adding either the I, IV, or V chord to give it structure.

Feel free to put intros and endings to songs that you feel could use them. Be sure to study the song structure and chord patterns in each song. At least 5 of the songs below, (*) you have already conquered. Have fun!!! Can you think of other songs?

When you have successfully conquered at least a dozen or more songs this way, you are then ready to take your ear-training to the next level – Intermediate!

Ready, set, go!

Easy Ear Song Categories to Learn

1. Nursery Rhymes
2. Patriotic
3. Sunday School
4. Pre-school/School songs
5. Some hymns/sacred/traditional
6. Weddings/Funerals
7. Praise & Worship/Contemporary
8. Seasonal Holiday songs
9. Birthday songs

(Categorized)

Nursery Rhymes

1. Wheels on the Bus
2. This Old Man
3. Mary Had A Little Lamb
4. London Bridge
5. Itsy Bitsy Spider
6. Found A Peanut
7. Three Blind Mice
8. Row, Row, Row Your Boat
9. The Farmer and the Dell
10. Bingo
11. Yankee Doodle
12. Ode To Joy
13. Old McDonald Had A Farm
14. Hush Little Baby Don't You Cry

Patriotic Songs
1. This Land is Your Land
2. God Bless America
3. My Country Tis of Thee
4. Star-Spangled Banner
5. Lift Every Voice and Sing
6. America the Beautiful
7. We Shall Overcome

Sunday School/Pre-school/School
1. Oh When The Saints
2. Oh, How I Love Jesus
3. Victory Is Mine
4. What A Mighty God We Serve
5. Oh the Blood of Jesus
6. Kumba Ya, My Lord
7. This Little Light of Mine
8. In the Name of Jesus, We have the Victory
9. Little David Play On Your Harp
10. If You're Happy and You Know It
11. We Bring the Sacrifice of Praise
12. This is The Day
13. God is So Good
14. Yes, Jesus Loves Me
15. We Are, Climbing, Jacob's Ladder
16. Praise Him, Praise Him All Ye Little Children
17. I Will Bless Thee Oh Lord

Sacred Hymns
1. Amazing Grace
2. At The Cross
3. His Eye Is On The Sparrow
4. Leaning On the Everlasting Arm
5. Pass Me Not
6. What A Friend
7. How Great Thou Art
8. Old Rugged Cross
9. Just A Closer Walk With Thee
10. I Need Thee

Christmas Songs
1. Ode To Joy
2. Joy To The World
3. Silent Night
4. Frosty The Snowman
5. Noel
6. Jolly Old Saint Nicholas
7. Santa Clause Is Coming To Town
8. We Wish You A Merry Christmas
9. Away In A Manger
10. Silver Bells

Glossary/Answers

To Fill – In Songs

Printed in Great Britain
by Amazon

57700652R00043